CATS SET I

MAINE COON CATS

Tamara L. Britton
ABDO Publishing Company

visit us at
www.abdopublishing.com

Published by ABDO Publishing Company, 8000 West 78th Street, Edina, Minnesota 55439. Copyright © 2011 by Abdo Consulting Group, Inc. International copyrights reserved in all countries. No part of this book may be reproduced in any form without written permission from the publisher. The Checkerboard Library™ is a trademark and logo of ABDO Publishing Company.

Printed in the United States of America, North Mankato, Minnesota.
042010
092010

PRINTED ON RECYCLED PAPER

Cover Photo: Peter Arnold
Interior Photos: Alamy p. 21; Photo by Helmi Flick pp. 5, 9, 10, 11, 13, 16–17; iStockphoto pp. 6–7; Peter Arnold pp. 14, 15, 18, 19

Editor: BreAnn Rumsch
Art Direction & Cover Design: Neil Klinepier

Library of Congress Cataloging-in-Publication Data

Britton, Tamara L., 1963-
  Maine coon cats / Tamara L. Britton.
      p. cm. -- (Cats)
  Includes index.
  ISBN 978-1-61613-398-6
  1. Maine coon cat--Juvenile literature. I. Title.
  SF449.M34B75 2011
  636.8'3--dc22
                                      2010013215

CONTENTS

LIONS, TIGERS, AND CATS

Cats are members of the family **Felidae**. There are 37 species in this family. Lions, tigers, and **domestic** cats are all members of this family.

Today's domestic cats have a long history. Their ancestors are African wildcats. About 3,500 years ago, ancient Egyptians began to tame wildcats. The cats kept rats and mice out of the buildings where grain harvests were stored.

Soon, other societies recognized the importance of cats. From Africa, these animals spread to Europe and North and South America. Today, more than 40 different **breeds** of domestic cats exist worldwide.

Maine coon cats

MAINE COON CATS

The Maine coon cat is native to the state of Maine. Early settlers brought short-haired cats to the area. Later, long-haired cats arrived on merchant ships from Europe. The two cat types mated, and their descendants became Maine coon cats.

The Maine coon cat has a long, weather-resistant coat and a sturdy body. These features allowed it to survive harsh winters. Mainers admired these tough cats for their mousing skills. Intelligence and a good nature made the cats even more popular.

In 1895, a Maine coon cat won first place and best in show at a cat show in New York City, New York. Beginning in 1897, a Maine coon cat won a Boston, Massachusetts, cat show three years in a row!

The Maine coon cat is Maine's official state cat!

But in time, the Maine coon cat fell from favor with cat lovers. The cats became scarce. Some people believed the **breed** was extinct! Then in 1950, admirers began working to save it.

In 1976, their hard work paid off. That year, the Maine coon cat became recognized by the **Cat Fanciers' Association (CFA)**. Two years later, the CFA grand champion and best of breed was a Maine coon cat. Today, the breed is the CFA's third most popular.

QUALITIES

Maine coon cats are sturdy, gentle, and loyal animals. They are also sweet, loving pets. In fact, they get along well with kids and dogs!

These easygoing, affectionate cats like to be around their people. They will hang out with their owners and help with any projects that are in progress. But, Maine coon cats are not lap cats! While they love to socialize, they remain independent.

Maine coon cats also have big personalities! They live to play, even when they are older. These big cats are also very vocal. They communicate with high-pitched chirps and mews.

Maine coon cats can seem like kittens in cat bodies! Toys will encourage their playful nature.

COAT AND COLOR

Maine coon cats have long, shaggy coats. The **breed** developed this thick coat for protection against harsh New England winters. The coat protects the cat from rain, snow, and cold.

Today, this coat is a well-recognized Maine coon cat feature! It is long and full on the cat's chest, stomach, and rear end. It is shorter on the shoulders and the back. This keeps the hair from becoming caught on brush and shrubs.

Maine coon cat coats come in many different colors. The

A solid white Maine coon cat's coat is both protective and beautiful.

10

Calico Maine coon cats are white with red and black patches.

solid colors are white, black, blue, red, and cream. The combination colors include solid, **tabby**, tabby and white, **bicolored**, and **parti-colored**. There are three coat patterns. They are classic, mackerel, and patched.

Most Maine coon cats have brown tabby coats. Their eyes can be shades of green, gold, or copper. White Maine coon cats may have blue eyes, or two eyes of different colors!

SIZE

The Maine coon cat is a large cat with a muscular body. Males weigh between 12 and 18 pounds (5 and 7 kg). Females are smaller, ranging from 9 to 12 pounds (4 to 5 kg).

A Maine coon cat has a deep, broad chest. Its legs are medium length and straight. Large, round, tufted feet act like snowshoes when the cat is out in the winter. The long, bushy tail wraps around the cat to keep it warm.

The cat's head is slightly longer than it is wide. It features high cheekbones and a square **muzzle**. The Maine coon cat's large, wide-set eyes are oval shaped. They slant slightly up toward the base of the ears. The ears are large, tapered, and well tufted. The taper and tuft make them appear pointed!

A female Maine coon cat (left)
is smaller than a male (right).

CARE

Cats are naturally clean. They use their rough tongues to wash their fur. But, Maine coon cats have a lot of fur! So, they should be brushed weekly to remove loose hair. This will keep them from swallowing hair and forming hairballs.

Cats also have a natural instinct to bury their waste. So, you can train your Maine coon cat to use a **litter box**. You will need to remove waste from the box daily. And, the box should be in a quiet place away from the cat's food and water.

Maine coon cats need to sharpen their claws. A scratching post keeps furniture and carpet safe from damage!

Vaccines may look scary, but they are very important.

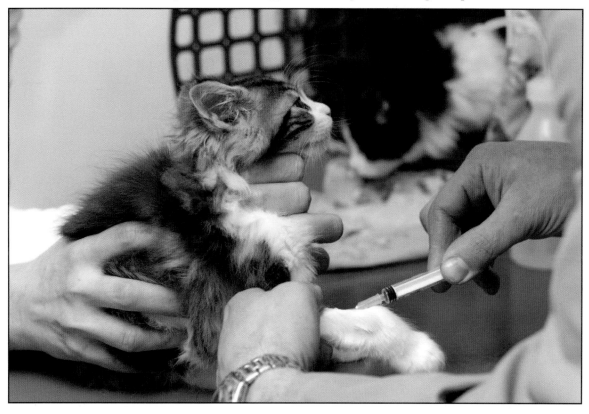

Maine coon cats are solid, rugged cats. However, they can develop health problems such as heart and hip trouble. A good relationship with a veterinarian is important. He or she can provide yearly checkups and **vaccines**. The veterinarian can also **spay** or **neuter** your cat.

FEEDING

Cats are carnivores. So, they need meat in their diets. You will need to feed your Maine coon cat food that contains protein, such as beef, poultry, or fish. Good cat food contains all the **nutrients** your cat needs.

The three kinds of commercial cat food are dry, semimoist, and

canned. Each type offers different recipes based on age, weight, and health.

The food label will tell you how much to feed your pet, and how often. If you are concerned about your cat's weight, check with your veterinarian. He or she can recommend a healthy diet.

With a proper diet, fresh water, and regular exercise, Maine coon kittens will grow into healthy cats!

Maine coon cats also need plenty of fresh water. Make sure to have some available at all times. Many cats also enjoy an occasional treat.

Kittens

A Maine coon cat can reproduce when it is 7 to 12 months old. After mating, the female is **pregnant** for about 65 days. She may have three **litters** each year. Each litter will have about four kittens.

The kittens are born blind and deaf. Their senses begin to function when they are two weeks old. Maine coon cat kittens begin to play and explore within their first three weeks. By then, they can see and hear. And, their teeth begin to come in.

Kittens drink their mother's milk until they are about five weeks old.

When the kittens are 12 to 16 weeks old, they can go home with new families. Maine coon cats develop slowly. They will not be fully mature until 3 to 4 years of age.

All kittens are born with blue eyes. Some keep that eye color as adults. For other kittens, it begins to change within the first weeks of life.

Buying a Kitten

Do you think a Maine coon cat is the right cat for you? If so, look for a good **breeder**. Kittens are available from breeders when they are three to four months old. You may also find a Maine coon cat through a shelter or a rescue organization.

The cost of a Maine coon cat depends on such factors as its markings and **pedigree**. Kittens from award-winning parents may cost hundreds of dollars. When you buy a Maine coon cat, you should file its pedigree papers with the **CFA**.

When buying a kitten, check it closely for signs of good health. Its ears, nose, mouth, and fur should be clean. The eyes should be bright and clear. The cat should be alert and interested in its surroundings. With **purebred** cats, how the parents behave can indicate a kitten's future behavior.

A Maine coon cat will be a loving companion for 10 to 15 years.

GLOSSARY

bicolored - having two colors.

breed - a group of animals sharing the same ancestors and appearance. A breeder is a person who raises animals. Raising animals is often called breeding them.

Cat Fanciers' Association (CFA) - a group that sets the standards for judging all breeds of cats.

domestic - tame, especially relating to animals.

Felidae (FEHL-uh-dee) - the scientific Latin name for the cat family. Members of this family are called felids. They include domestic cats, lions, tigers, leopards, jaguars, cougars, wildcats, lynx, and cheetahs.

litter - all of the kittens born at one time to a mother cat.

litter box - a box filled with cat litter, which is similar to sand. Cats use litter boxes to bury their waste.

muzzle - an animal's nose and jaws.

neuter (NOO-tuhr) - to remove a male animal's reproductive organs.

nutrient - a substance found in food and used in the body. It promotes growth, maintenance, and repair.

parti-colored - having a dominant color broken up by patches of one or more other colors.

pedigree - a record of an animal's ancestors.

pregnant - having one or more babies growing within the body.

purebred - an animal whose parents are both from the same breed.

spay - to remove a female animal's reproductive organs.

tabby - a coat pattern featuring stripes or splotches of a dark color on a lighter background. Individual hairs are banded with light and dark colors.

vaccine (vak-SEEN) - a shot given to prevent illness or disease.

WEB SITES

To learn more about Maine coon cats, visit ABDO Publishing Company on the World Wide Web at **www.abdopublishing.com**. Web sites about Maine coon cats are featured on our Book Links page. These links are routinely monitored and updated to provide the most current information available.

INDEX